# CRAZY
# GOOD
## CLEAN
# JOKES

▲▲▲▲▲▲▲▲▲▲▲▲▲▲▲▲▲▲

## FOR KIDS!
### Bob Phillips

*Illustrations by*
*Norm Daniels*

**HARVEST HOUSE PUBLISHERS**
Eugene, Oregon 97402

**CRAZY GOOD CLEAN JOKES FOR KIDS!**

Copyright © 1994 by Harvest House Publishers
Eugene, Oregon 97402

Library of Congress Cataloging-in-Publication Data

Phillips, Bob, 1940-
    Crazy good clean jokes for kids / Bob Phillips.
        p.  m.
    ISBN 1-56507-208-1
    1. Wit and humor, Juvenile.  [1. Riddles.  2. Jokes.]  I. Title.
PN6163.P482    1994                                             93-39053
818'.5402—dc20                                                      CIP
                                                                   AC

**Printed in the United States of America.**

94  95  96  97  98  99  00  01 — 10  9  8  7  6  5  4  3  2  1

*To the
clearly cool,
cracked, and crazy
Cross family.*

# Contents

# Cracked 'n' Crazy

What kind of ears does a crazy engine have?
*Engineers.*

•

Where does a crazy Ken doll grill his hamburgers?
*On a Barbie-cue.*

•

How can you tell if your crazy lawn is sick?
*When you hear the grass mown.*

•

When the crazy baby cries at night, who gets up?
*The whole neighborhood.*

•

What is a conversation among crazy dogs called?
*A bowwow powwow.*

•

Why are crazy oysters lazy?
*Because they are always found in beds.*

•

What is a stupid ruler called?
*A ding-a-ling king.*

•

What two letters got kicked out of the crazy alphabet for
being rotten?
*D-K.*

•

Who is Mexico's most famous fat man?
*Pauncho Villa.*

•

When does a crazy girl admire a bachelor's voice?
*When there is a ring in it.*

•

What's the best way to find out what a crazy woman
  thinks of you?
*Marry her.*

•

Why do crazy hummingbirds hum?
*Because they can't remember the words.*

# Curtis &
# Cassandra Crazy

Cassandra: What's wrong with overeating?
Curtis: Search me.
Cassandra: It makes you thick to your stomach.

•

Cassandra: When does a crazy farmer have the best chance to see his pigs?
Curtis: You've got me guessing.
Cassandra: When he has a sty on his eye.

•

Cassandra: Why does a crazy elephant like peanuts?
Curtis: I'm not sure.
Cassandra: Because it can look in the wrappers for prizes.

•

Cassandra: Why was the crazy fish turned down by the army?
Curtis: How should I know?
Cassandra: He failed his herring test.

•

Cassandra: What do you get when you cross a crazy lighthouse and a henhouse?
Curtis: Beats me.
Cassandra: Beacon and eggs.

•

Cassandra: What does a crazy nearsighted gingerbread man use for eyes?
Curtis: I can't guess.
Cassandra: Contact raisins.

•

Cassandra: What do you get when you cross a crazy movie with a swimming pool?
Curtis: I have no clue.
Cassandra: A dive-in theater.

•

Cassandra: What crazy shampoo do mountains use?
Curtis: Give me the answer.
Cassandra: Head and Boulders.

•

Cassandra: What part of the crazy car is first to get weary?
Curtis: I don't know.
Cassandra: The tire.

•

Cassandra: What is yellow, swims in the ocean, and swallows ships?
Curtis: I have no idea.
Cassandra: Moby Banana.

•

Cassandra: What did the crazy adding machine say to the clerk?
Curtis: You tell me.
Cassandra: You can count on me.

•

Cassandra: What did the crazy apple tree say to the farmer?
Curtis: I give up.
Cassandra: Why don't you stop picking on me?

•

Cassandra: What is the smallest building in all of Crazyland?
Curtis: Who knows?
Cassandra: The Hall of Fame.

•

Cassandra: What do crazy crows sail in?
Curtis: That's a mystery.
Cassandra: Crowboats.

# 3

# *Crazy As a Loon*

What is smaller than a crazy ant's mouth?
*His teeth.*

•

How does a crazy person spell "farm"?
*E-I-E-I-O.*

•

How does a crazy musician brush his teeth?
*With a tuba toothpaste.*

•

How does a crazy train conductor sneeze?
*Ahhhh choo-choo!*

•

How can you recognize crazy rabbit stew?
*It has hares in it.*

•

How many crazy actors does it take to change a light
    bulb?
*One hundred. One to change it, and 99 to stand around and
    say, "I could have done that."*

•

What goes putt-putt-putt-putt?
*An over-par golfer.*

•

What do you call someone who steals pigs?
*A hamburglar.*

•

What did the crazy sea say to the shore?
*Nothing. It just waved.*

•

What two things can you never eat for breakfast?
*Lunch and dinner.*

•

Why did the crazy little boy go to sleep with birds in his shoes?
*He wanted to feed his pigeon toes.*

•

How should you greet a crazy German barber?
*Herr Dresser.*

•

Why is a crazy ex-boxer like a beehive?
*An ex-boxer is an ex-pounder; an expounder is a commentator; a common tater is an Irish tater; an Irish tater is a speck'd tater; a spectator is a beholder; and a beeholder is a beehive.*

•

Which is larger, crazy Mr. Larger or crazy Mr. Larger's baby?
*The baby is a little Larger.*

•

If joy is the opposite of sorrow, what is the opposite of woe?
*Giddyap!*

•

What did one crazy elevator say to the other crazy elevator?
*I think I'm coming down with something.*

# 4

## Completely Crazy

Who sings "Love Me Tender" and makes crazy Christmas toys?
*Santa's little Elvis.*

•

What is the right kind of timber for building crazy castles in the air?
*Sunbeams.*

•

How did the prime minister of Crazyland deal with the problem of Red China?
*He bought a pink tablecloth.*

•

Which season do crazy kangaroos like the best?
*Springtime!*

•

Where are ankles located?
*Overshoes.*

•

Where do crazy fish keep their life savings?
*In a riverbank.*

•

What do you call a crazy raccoon that wears bow ties?
*Tycoon.*

•

What do you call it when your crazy toes have a good cry?
*Football.*

•

Why is *E* the most unfortunate of all the letters?
*Because it is never in cash, always in debt, and never out of
danger.*

•

What two crazy numbers multiplied together make 13?
*One and 13.*

•

Why shouldn't crazy American girls learn Russian?
*Because one tongue is enough for any girl.*

•

What gets lost every time you stand up?
*Your lap.*

•

If a soft answer turneth away wrath, what does a hard
answer do for you?
*It turneth wrath your way.*

•

How can you tell a crazy Jersey cow from any other cow?
*By its license plate.*

•

What is the longest word in the dictionary?
*Smiles. There's a mile between the first and last letter.*

# 5

# *Clem & Carmen Crazy*

Clem: Why did the crazy otter cross the road?
Carmen: Beats me.
Clem: He didn't want to be mistaken for a chicken.

•

Clem: Why couldn't the crazy crab learn to share?
Carmen: I can't guess.
Clem: Because it was shellfish.

•

Clem: What is the crazy sheep's favorite comic strip?
Carmen: I have no clue.
Clem: Mutton Jeff.

•

Clem: What is the difference between a crazy lizard, a
crybaby, and Roadrunner?
Carmen: I don't know.
Clem: One creeps, one weeps, and one beeps.

•

Clem: What did the crazy thief name his son?
Carmen: I have no idea.
Clem: Robin.

•

Clem: What is impossible to hold for half an hour, even
   though it's lighter than air?
Carmen: You tell me.
Clem: Your breath.

•

Clem: What do you find in a crazy pig mall?
Carmen: You've got me.
Clem: Pork shops.

•

Clem: What is the world's craziest satellite?
Carmen: It's unknown to me.
Clem: A fool moon.

•

Clem: What crazy ape helped settle the American frontier?
Carmen: I give up.
Clem: Daniel Ba-Boone.

•

Clem: What do you call crazy short stories written by hogs?
Carmen: Who knows?
Clem: Pig tales.

•

Clem: What do 500-pound canaries do on Sundays?
Carmen: My mind is a blank.
Clem: They go to chirp.

•

Clem: What is the best-looking geometric figure?
Carmen: That's a mystery.
Clem: Acute angle.

•

Clem: What do you get when you use crazy soap and water on the stove?
Carmen: Tell me.
Clem: Foam on the range.

•

Clem: What is the craziest and cheapest way to buy holes?
Carmen: I don't have the foggiest.
Clem: Wholesale.

# 6

# *Constantly Crazy*

What can overpower a crazy karate master without hurting him?
*Sleep.*

•

Why doesn't the crazy sheik get married?
*Harem-scarem.*

•

How many letters are in the alphabet?
*Eleven. T-H-E  A-L-P-H-A-B-E-T.*

•

What kind of crazy dress do you have but never wear?
*Your address.*

•

Why do crazy single girls like the moon?
*Because there's a man in it.*

•

What crazy vegetable do you find in crowded streetcars
and buses?
*Squash.*

•

What do you do when you want to take a pole from one
place to another?
*Totem pole.*

•

Where do crazy plants grow?
*In crackpots.*

•

What has no feet but always wears shoes?
*The sidewalk.*

•

What does the crazy envelope say when you lick it?
*It just shuts up and says nothing.*

•

To what question must you positively answer, "Yes"?
*What does Y-E-S spell?*

•

Why is a crazy pig in your kitchen like a house on fire?
*The sooner you put it out, the better.*

# Cool 'n' Crazy

What makes more noise than a crazy pig in a sty?
*Two pigs.*

•

How do you top a crazy car?
*Tep on the brake, tupid!*

•

Which crazy fruit is always sad?
*Blueberries.*

•

Where do crazy peroxide blondes sit at baseball games?
*In the bleachers.*

•

I have leaves, but I'm not a plant. What am I?
*A table.*

•

What's crazy, hard-boiled, and can bench press 600
   pounds?
*Arnold Schwarzenegg.*

•

With what two crazy animals do you always go to bed?
*Two calves.*

•

What is the difference between an engineer and a teacher?
*One minds the train, while the other trains the mind.*

•

What do you do with a crazy blue monster?
*Cheer him up.*

•

What crazy country makes you shiver with cold?
*Chile.*

•

What crazy fish is man's best friend?
*The dogfish.*

•

What do you call the secret instructions for opening a
   zipper?
*A zip code.*

•

Why was crazy Cleopatra so hard to get along with?
*She was the queen of denial.*

•

Name a crazy carpenter's tool you can spell forward and
   backward the same way.
*Level.*

# 8

## *Claude & Candice Crazy*

Candice: Who was the famous rooster who rode with the crazy Rough Riders and later became president?
Claude: Beats me.
Candice: Teddy Roostervelt.

•

Candice: Where do crazy frogs hang up their coats?
Claude: I can't guess.
Candice: In the croak room.

•

Candice: Why did Crazy Elsie the Cow go to Hollywood?
Claude: I have no clue.
Candice: To be a moo-vie star.

•

Candice: Why don't crazy rabbits need calculators?
Claude: I don't know.
Candice: Because they can multiply quickly without them.

•

Candice: What crazy game do rabbits always love to play?
Claude: You tell me.
Candice: Hopscotch.

•

Candice: What's black and white and pink all over?
Claude: I give up.
Candice: An embarrassed zebra.

•

Candice: What crazy cowboy steals teapots?
Claude: That's a mystery.
Candice: A kettle rustler.

•

Candice: What crazy business is King Kong in?
Claude: Who knows?
Candice: Monkey business.

•

Candice: What crazy word of three syllables is always mispronounced?
Claude: I have no idea.
Candice: Mispronounced.

•

Candice: What do crazy, short fairy-tale characters wear to look taller?
Claude: You've got me.
Candice: Rumple-stilts.

•

Candice: What crazy dancer spins straw into gold?
Claude: My mind is a blank.
Candice: Rhumba-stiltskin.

•

Candice: What did crazy Ali Baba write on?
Claude: Tell me.
Candice: Sandpaper.

•

Candice: What state would a gold prospector like?
Claude: It's unknown to me.
Candice: Ore.

•

Candice: What state do you use when you talk about yourself?
Claude: I don't have the foggiest.
Candice: Me.

•

Candice: What state is a church service?
Claude: I'm in the dark.
Candice: Mass.

•

Candice: What did crazy Sir Lancelot wear to bed?
Claude: Search me.
Candice: A knightgown.

# 9

# *Crackpot Crazies*

Who haunts the Sahara Desert?
*The sandwich.*

•

Where does crazy Mother Goose leave her garbage?
*At the Humpty Dump.*

•

Who helped crazy Cinderella's cat go to the ball?
*Its furry godmother.*

•

Where do crazy dieters go on vacation?
*Hungary.*

•

Do you know the crazy joke about the oil?
*Well, I won't tell you. It's too crude.*

•

What do you get when you cross crazy peanuts with golf
balls?
*Peanut putter.*

•

What happened when the crazy dog visited the flea circus?
*He stole the show.*

•

Why does a crazy hen lay an egg?
*Because she can't lay a brick.*

•

Why is it hard to talk with a crazy goat around?
*Because he always butts in.*

•

How do you spell mousetrap using three letters?
*C-A-T.*

•

I came to town and met three crazy people. They were neither men, nor women, nor children. What were they?
*A man, a woman, and a child.*

•

What crazy animal has the highest level of intelligence?
*The giraffe.*

•

What is so brittle that it can be broken just by naming it?
*Silence.*

•

What kind of crazy sea creature is like an expression of disbelief?
*Abalone.*

# Cream of the Crazies

I have a mouth, but no teeth. What am I?
*A river.*

•

Who is the first crazy Irishman you see in the spring?
*Patty O'Furniture.*

•

How do crazy baby birds learn how to fly?
*They just sort of wing it.*

•

How do crazy soldiers sleep out in the open?
*In beds of flowers under sheets of rain and blankets of fog.*

•

What's beneath your crazy nose?
*Tulips.*

•

If a woman married crazy Mr. Hill, whose brother has
children, what would she become?
*Ant Hill.*

•

If your crazy aunt had rabbit ears, what would she be?
*Antenna.*

•

What does a crazy hen do just before she stands on one
   foot?
*She lifts up the other one.*

•

What do you call someone with a crazy burning desire?
*An arsonist.*

•

What is another name for a crazy maternity dress?
*A space suit.*

•

Why would you expect a crazy fisherman to be more honest than a shepherd?
*Because a fisherman lives by hook and a shepherd lives by crook.*

•

What is the most crazy and popular gardening magazine?
*Weeder's Digest.*

•

What makes a crazy, empty matchbox superior to any other?
*It is matchless.*

•

How often do crazy ocean liners sink?
*Only once.*

•

When is it bad luck to have a crazy black cat follow you?
*When you are a mouse.*

# Cornelius &
# Claudia Crazy

Cornelius: What is found in the center of America and
Australia?
Claudia: Beats me.
Cornelius: The letter *R*.

•

Cornelius: What are 365 periods of disappointment
called?
Claudia: I can't guess.
Cornelius: A year.

•

Cornelius: Why didn't crazy Eve have any sisters?
Claudia: I have no clue.
Cornelius: Because Adam had no spare ribs.

•

Cornelius: Why is it a good idea to have holes in your
jeans?
Claudia: I don't know.
Cornelius: So that you can get your legs inside.

•

Cornelius: What is a crazy cat's skin used for?
Claudia: I have no idea.
Cornelius: To hold the cat together.

•

Cornelius: What is incredibly intelligent, weighs 200
  pounds, and is made out of iron?
Claudia: You tell me.
Cornelius: Albert Einstein Dumbbell.

•

Cornelius: What climbs trees, stores nuts for the winter,
  and weighs three tons?
Claudia: I give up.
Cornelius: A crazy elephant who thinks he is a squirrel.

•

Cornelius: What crazy locomotive wears sneakers?
Claudia: Who knows?
Cornelius: A shoe-shoe train.

•

Cornelius: What do you call great bodies of water filled
  with grape juice?
Claudia: That's a mystery.
Cornelius: The Grape Lakes.

•

Cornelius: What do crazy patriotic monkeys wave on
  Flag Day?
Claudia: Tell me.
Cornelius: Star-Spangled bananas.

•

Cornelius: What is harder than catching a crazy train when you're late?
Claudia: I don't have the foggiest.
Cornelius: Throwing one.

•

Cornelius: What happens to crazy Whistler's mother when she works too hard?
Claudia: It's unknown to me.
Cornelius: She goes off her rocker.

•

Cornelius: What kind of car does Crazy Elsie the Cow drive?
Claudia: My mind is a blank.
Cornelius: A moo-ving van.

•

Cornelius: What crazy state is necessary for dirty clothes?
Claudia: I'm in the dark.
Cornelius: Wash.

•

Cornelius: What is it called when you holler to a crazy person two miles away?
Claudia: Search me.
Cornelius: Lung distance.

# 12

# *Catalog of Craziness*

Did you hear about the crazy football captain who didn't believe he lost the coin toss and demanded to see it again on instant replay?

•

When five crazy men fell in the water, why did only four of them get their hair wet?
*Because one of them was bald.*

•

Sign on a newly seeded lawn:
*Your feet are killing me!*

•

Sign in a crazy old-folks home:
*We're not deaf; we have already heard everything worth hearing.*

•

Sign in a crazy shop window:
*Wanted: Clerk to work eight hours a day to replace one who didn't.*

•

Sign in a crazy delicatessen window:
*Come in for a hello and good buys.*

•

Sign in a crazy ice-cream shop:
*You can't beat our milk shakes, but you can lick our ice cream.*

•

A crazy rope tried to enlist in the army, but the recruiting sergeant rejected it on sight. "No ropes allowed," he said.

The crazy rope went home, tied itself into a big knot, and frayed itself at both ends. The next day it returned to the recruiting office.

"Hey, aren't you the crazy rope that tried to enlist yesterday?" asked the sergeant.

"No," said the crazy rope, "I'm a frayed knot."

•

Crazy Clive: Have you ever seen a crazy catfish?
Cynthia: Of course.
Crazy Clive: How did he hold the pole?

•

Crazy Cleaver: I was once a 90-pound weakling. When I went to the beach, a 200-pound bully kicked sand in my face. That was the end. I exercised every day and in a little while I weighed 200 pounds.
Claudia: Then what happened?
Crazy Cleaver: I went to the beach and a 400-pound bully kicked sand in my face!

•

Sergeant: So you're complaining about a little sand in your soup?

Crazy private: Yes, sir.

Sergeant: Did you join the army to serve your country or complain about the food?

Crazy private: I joined the army to serve my country, not to eat it.

•

If you breathe oxygen during the daytime, what do you breathe at nighttime?

*Nitrogen, of course!*

•

Crazy Collette: A strange thing happened to me out in the street. A bum came up to me and asked me for a quarter to eat.

Connley: That's not strange. Bums do that all the time. Did you give him a quarter?

Crazy Collette: Yeah. And he ate it!

•

Instead of bringing the teacher an apple every day, crazy David, the baker's son, brought her a pretzel. One day she said to him, "These pretzels are good, but please tell your dad that they are a little too salty for me."

The next day, she received a pretzel with no salt on it. From then on the pretzels arrived without salt. A month later she said to crazy David, "I hope your father doesn't go through too much trouble making these pretzels without salt."

"He doesn't make 'em without salt," said the boy. "I lick it off."

•

Sign in a crazy egg factory:
*Fowl play not allowed.*

•

Sign in a crazy pawnbroker's shop:
*See us at your earliest inconvenience.*

•

Crazy Saint Peter greeted a lawyer at the pearly gates
with unusual warmth.

"Gee," said the lawyer, "does everyone get this kind of
treatment?"

"You're not just anyone," crazy Saint Peter replied. "We
seldom get lawyers who are as distinguished and old as
you."

"But I'm only 48," said the lawyer.

"Funny," said crazy Saint Peter. "You have billed for so
many hours we thought you were 80."

•

How can you tell when a crazy tree is truly frightened?
*When it is petrified.*

# 13

# Certified Crazy

How do you cheer a crazy basketball player?
*Hoop, hoop, hooray!*

•

What day of the year is a command to go forward?
*March fourth.*

•

How do you revive a crazy butterfly that has fainted?
*With moth-to-moth resuscitation.*

•

Who invents crazy telephones and carries your luggage?
*Alexander Graham Bellhop.*

•

Who was crazy Peeping Tom's sister?
*Little Bo Peeping.*

•

What would you get if you dropped chocolate on the beach?
*Sandy candy.*

•

What is the best way to keep a crazy skunk from smelling?
*Hold his nose.*

•

If a crazy man married a princess, what would he be?
*Her husband.*

•

When was crazy beef the highest it has ever been?
*When the cow jumped over the moon.*

•

What did the crazy Eskimo shout to his dogs, Corn and Meal?
*Cornmeal mush!*

•

If all the money in the world were divided equally among
the crazy people, how much would each person get?
*An equal amount.*

•

What do they call a crazy dollar with all the taxes taken
  out?
*A nickel.*

•

What kind of crazy jokes does a scholar make?
*Wisecracks.*

•

If the crazy man you work for weighs 2,000 pounds, what
  do you call him?
*Boston (boss ton).*

•

What is the best day to fry crazy food?
*Friday.*

•

What two opposites mean the same thing?
*Half-full and half-empty.*

# 14

## *Conrad &*
## *Camilla Crazy*

Camilla: When can you spell "crazy" using just one letter?
Conrad: Beats me.
Camilla: When it's *U*!

•

Camilla: Which crazy traffic light is the bravest?
Conrad: I can't guess.
Camilla: The one that doesn't turn yellow.

•

Camilla: Why did the crazy frog get kicked out of the navy?
Conrad: I don't know.
Camilla: He kept jumping ship.

•

Camilla: What are the odds of something crazy happening at 12:50 P.M.?
Conrad: I have no idea.
Camilla: Ten-to-one.

•

Camilla: What is the biggest soda in the world?
Conrad: You tell me.
Camilla: Minnesota.

•

Camilla: What happens to crazy dogs who chase cars?
Conrad: Who knows?
Camilla: They end up exhausted.

•

Camilla: What cultivates the earth and gives milk?
Conrad: You've got me.
Camilla: Bossie the Plow.

•

Camilla: Why did the crazy frog sit on the lily pad?
Conrad: I have no clue.
Camilla: Her sofa was being repaired.

•

Camilla: What does a crazy Eskimo put on his bed?
Conrad: My mind is a blank.
Camilla: A sheet of ice and a blanket of snow.

•

Camilla: What has brown fur, wears a ranger's hat, and
hangs from a tree?
Conrad: That's a mystery.
Camilla: Smokey Pear.

•

Camilla: What's another name for a crazy dining car?
Conrad: Tell me.
Camilla: A chew-chew train.

•

Camilla: What is orange and half a mile high?
Conrad: I don't have the foggiest.
Camilla: The Empire State Carrot.

•

Camilla: What did you do last summer?
Conrad: I worked for an elevator company.
Camilla: I'll bet that had its ups and downs.

•

Camilla: What crazy state is a doctor?
Conrad: I'm in the dark.
Camilla: MD.

•

Camilla: What crazy fruit studies for exams in a hurry?
Conrad: Search me.
Camilla: Cram-berries.

# 15

# *Chock-Full of Craziness*

Which crazy shoes are made for lazy people?
*Loafers.*

•

Was crazy Ben Franklin surprised when he discovered electricity?
*Oh yes, he was shocked.*

•

When crazy fish swim in schools, who helps out the teacher?
*The herring aid.*

•

When does crazy rainfall make mistakes?
*During a blunderstorm.*

•

What happens when the crazy bridge of your nose collapses?
*Nose drops.*

•

Why couldn't the crazy pony talk?
*He was a little horse.*

•

Do crazy fish sing?
*Only when they have musical scales.*

•

Why was it that after crazy Mrs. Jones had given her
neighbor a butter churn, her neighbor gave another
one back?
*One good churn deserves another.*

•

Why does a crazy elephant wear sunglasses?
*If you were the one they were telling all these jokes about, you
would want to hide, too!*

•

Why did the crazy shrimp blush?
*Because someone saw it in the salad dressing.*

•

Why is an empty purse always the same?
*Because there is never any change in it.*

•

If a crazy farmer sold 500 bushels of wheat for a dollar a
　bushel, what would he get?
*A lot of customers.*

•

If one crazy horse is shut up in a stable and another one is
　running loose down the road, which horse is singing
　"Don't Fence Me In"?
*Neither! Horses can't sing.*

•

What will change a crazy pear into a pearl?
*The letter L.*

•

What do you call a crazy veterinarian with laryngitis?
*A hoarse doctor.*

•

If a crazy cannibal ate his mother's sister, what would he
　be?
*An aunt eater.*

# 16

## *Clearly Crazy*

What is the difference between a crazy mouse and a young lady?
*One harms the cheese, and the other charms the he's.*

•

How does a crazy person fan himself?
*He holds his hand still and waves his face in front of it.*

•

Where do crazy pickles party?
*In a barrel of fun.*

•

Which is heavier, a half moon or a full moon?
*A half moon, because the full moon is lighter.*

•

A successful criminal:
*A smug thug.*

•

What kind of crazy sentence would you get if you broke
   the law of gravity?
*A suspended one.*

•

What has never killed anyone, but seems to scare some
   people half to death?
*Work.*

•

An insane flower:
*A crazy daisy.*

•

What did the crazy mother ghost say to the baby ghost
   when they got in the car?
*Fasten your sheet belt.*

•

What is a crazy witch's favorite plant?
*Poison ivy.*

•

Who is the oldest whistler in the world?
*The wind.*

•

Do crazy chickens jog?
*No, but turkeys trot.*

•

If an apple a day keeps the crazy doctor away, what does
　an onion do?
*It keeps everybody away.*

•

What is the oldest crazy tree?
*The elder.*

•

Why didn't the crazy baby get hurt when he fell down?
*Because he was wearing safety pins.*

# Clyde & Carlotta Crazy

Clyde: What is the best way to kill time?
Carlotta: I can't guess.
Clyde: Work it to death.

•

Clyde: Why was the crazy calendar so sad?
Carlotta: I have no clue.
Clyde: Its days were numbered.

•

Clyde: Why was the crazy duck unhappy?
Carlotta: I don't know.
Clyde: His bill was in the mail.

•

Clyde: What is a crazy frog asked when it enters a restaurant?
Carlotta: I have no idea.
Clyde: Croaking or noncroaking?

•

Clyde: What can you hold without touching it?
Carlotta: Beats me.
Clyde: Your breath.

•

Clyde: What kind of crazy house weighs the least?
Carlotta: You tell me.
Clyde: A lighthouse.

•

Clyde: What is green, red, orange, yellow, purple, brown, pink, and covered with polka dots?
Carlotta: I give up.
Clyde: A crazy woman dressed up for church.

•

Clyde: What does it say on the bottom of Coke bottles in Crazyland?
Carlotta: Who knows?
Clyde: Open other end.

•

Clyde: What do you call a crazy hot dog who always speaks his mind?
Carlotta: You've got me.
Clyde: A frank-furter.

•

Clyde: What time is it when twelve crazy dogs chase a cat?
Carlotta: My mind is a blank.
Clyde: Twelve after one.

•

Clyde: What do crazy mechanics do in aerobics class?
Carlotta: That's a mystery.
Clyde: Touch their tow trucks.

•

Clyde: What crazy turkey starred in *Gone with the Wind*?
Carlotta: I don't have the foggiest.
Clyde: Clark Gobble.

•

Clyde: What was Chicken Souperman's other name?
Carlotta: It's unknown to me.
Clyde: Cluck Kent.

•

Clyde: What is worse than a crazy turtle with claustrophobia?
Carlotta: I'm in the dark.
Clyde: An elephant with hay fever.

•

Clyde: What practical jokes do crazy mathematicians play?

Carlotta: Search me.

Clyde: Arithmetricks.

# 18

# *Cargo of Craziness*

Do you know why crazy people get only half an hour off for lunch?
*If they had an hour, they would have to be retrained.*

•

"I picked some of your apples," yelled the motorist as he drove away from the crazy farmer's orchard. "I didn't think you would mind."
"Not at all," yelled the crazy farmer after him. "I picked some of your car's tools from the trunk. I didn't think you would mind, either."

•

Mother: You should eat your vegetables. Green things are good for you.
Crazy Cramer: In that case, couldn't I have lime sherbet instead?

•

Sign on a vegetable stand:
*Our corn will tickle your taste buds and make you smile from ear to ear.*

•

His brain is so small, he isn't smart enough to get a job as
a clown in a flea circus.

•

Was the blimp crazy?
*Yes, it was a balloonatic.*

•

Clayton: Ouch! I just got a lump on my head.
Carrie: That's swell.

•

Clide: Write something on a piece of paper.
Cleo: OK, what next?
Clide: Fold it, put it on the floor, and put your foot on it.
Cleo: OK, now what?
Clide: I can tell you what is on the paper.
Cleo: What?
Clide: Your foot.

•

Sending a crazy youngster through college these days is educational. It teaches his parents how to do without a lot of things.

•

Street sweeper: Did it hurt when the street lamp fell on your head?
Crazy street cleaner: No, it was a light pole.

•

A crazy buddy of mine was always being kept after school. He spent so much time at school, they delivered his mail there.

•

Carley: The doctor is helping me lose weight with these three pills. This red one is for before dinner. That green one is for after dinner.
Carma: And what is the pink one for?
Carley: The pink one is dinner.

•

Sign in a power plant:
*We have the power to make you see the light.*

•

Crazy handyman: I need a total of 36 two-by-fours.
Sales clerk: How long?
Crazy handyman: Oh, a long time. I'm building a house!

•

My husband is such a hypochondriac, he puts cough syrup on his pancakes.

•

I knew a guy who was so dumb he thought a Band-Aid was a charitable organization for musicians.

•

Golfer: You're a lousy caddy! When we get back to the clubhouse, I'm going to make sure that you get fired.
Crazy caddy: That's OK with me. By the time we get back to the clubhouse I'll be old enough to get a regular job!

# 19

# *Case of the Crazies*

What is the biggest handicap in golf?
*Honesty.*

•

How many crazy people does it require to take a picture off a wall?
*Ten. One to hold the picture and nine to knock down the wall.*

•

Who changed crazy King Tut's diapers?
*His mummy.*

•

I have ears, but I can't hear. What am I?
*A cornstalk.*

•

What do most people give and few people take?
*Advice.*

•

Where do crazy king crabs live?
*In sand castles.*

•

What is the difference between a crazy elephant and a flea?
*A crazy elephant can have fleas, but a flea can't have elephants.*

•

How do you remove varnish?
*Take out the letter R and make it vanish.*

•

What age do most crazy girls wish to attain?
*Marriage.*

•

What do you call a crazy prankster who eats chili peppers
for dinner?
*A hot time in the old clown tonight.*

•

What is the difference between a crazy lawyer and a
  vulture?
*Frequent-flier miles.*

●

What does a crazy hippopotamus have that no other
  animal has?
*A baby hippopotamus.*

●

What is the value of the moon?
*Four quarters.*

# 20

# *Clifford &*
# *Cordelia Crazy*

Cordelia: What grows larger the more you take away?
Clifford: Beats me.
Cordelia: A hole.

•

Cordelia: How can you change a crazy pumpkin into another vegetable?
Clifford: I can't guess.
Cordelia: Throw it down onto the ground and it will become squash.

•

Cordelia: Why did Mr. and Mrs. Crazy Cat get married?
Clifford: I have no clue.
Cordelia: They were a purr-fect match.

•

Cordelia: Why didn't crazy Clara like the joke about the Grand Canyon?
Clifford: I don't know.
Cordelia: It was too deep.

•

Cordelia: What do crazy sharks eat with their peanut
    butter?
Clifford: I don't have the foggiest.
Cordelia: Jellyfish.

•

Cordelia: What crazy bear never bathes?
Clifford: I have no idea.
Cordelia: Winnie-the-Phew.

•

Cordelia: What crazy cow jumps off buildings for fun?
Clifford: You tell me.
Cordelia: A dairy devil.

•

Cordelia: What would you get if you crossed a crazy
    dentist with a military officer?
Clifford: I give up.
Cordelia: A drill sergeant.

•

Cordelia: What crazy cowboy never said a word?
Clifford: Who knows?
Cordelia: Quiet Earp.

•

Cordelia: What do you get from a crazy and forgetful cow?
Clifford: You've got me.
Cordelia: Milk of Amnesia.

•

Cordelia: What do you get from a crazy and funny cow?
Clifford: My mind is a blank.
Cordelia: Cream of wit.

•

Cordelia: What happened to crazy Little Bo Peep after she spent all day looking for her sheep?
Clifford: That's a mystery.
Cordelia: She was Little Bo Pooped.

•

Cordelia: What crazy snowstorm covered the Emerald City?
Clifford: Tell me.
Cordelia: The Blizzard of Oz.

•

Cordelia: What do you get when you cross a crazy sheep with a monkey?
Clifford: It's unknown to me.
Cordelia: A baa-boon.

•

Cordelia: What's the name of the world's best-known waterfall?
Clifford: I'm in the dark.
Cordelia: Rain.

•

Cordelia: What happens to crazy spoons when they work too hard?
Clifford: Search me.
Cordelia: They go stir crazy!

# 21

# Crackling Crazies

How many sides does a circle have?
*Two. The inside and the outside.*

●

Why don't they let crazy people operate elevators?
*They forget the route.*

●

Who serves a four-year term of office, signs documents,
and rattles?
*The President of the United Snakes.*

●

How do crazy amoebas break up with their girlfriends?
*They split.*

●

What does bigmouth William do when he hears a secret?
*William Tell.*

●

Name two people who were never wrong.
*Wilbur and Orville Wright.*

●

When do you put a mouse in your sister's bed?
*When you can't find a frog.*

•

What colors would you paint the sun and the wind?
*The sun rose and the wind blue.*

•

When a crazy librarian goes fishing, what does she use
   for bait?
*Bookworms.*

•

What did one crazy horse say to the other?
*I can't remember your mane, but your pace is familiar.*

•

Why should a crazy man never tell his secrets in a corn-
field?
*Because there are too many ears there, and they might be
shocked.*

•

Which is the best side of the bed to sleep on?
*The top side.*

•

What did one stuck-up person say to another?
*Nothing.*

•

How can you be sure the engine in your car isn't missing?
*Lift the hood and look in.*

•

Why did the crazy whale cross the road?
*To get to the other tide.*

# 22

# *Crazy Doctors*

Doc, one night I dreamed I was in a wigwam, the next night I dreamed I was living in a teepee. What's happening to me?
*Nothing. You're just two tents (too tense).*

•

Doc, what's your best suggestion for this terrible breath I have?
*Lockjaw.*

•

Doc, I can't sleep at night. What should I do?
*Sleep during the day.*

•

Doc, what do you charge for a visit?
*I charge $50 for the first visit and $25 for each visit thereafter.*
Well I'm here again.
*Fine, then just take the same prescription I gave last time.*

•

Doc, this ointment you gave me makes my arm smart.
*Why not rub some on your head?*

•

Worried mother: My little boy just swallowed a bottle of
ink. What shall I do?
Crazy doctor: Try to get him to swallow a blotter!

•

Crazy patient: My doctor classified me as a workaholic
and suggested I get psychiatric treatment.
Friend: So what did you do?
Crazy patient: I got another job so I could afford a
psychiatrist.

•

Nurse: There is a man outside with a wooden leg named
Smith.
Crazy doctor: What is the name of his other leg?

•

Two crazy psychiatrists ran into each other on the street. One said to the other, "You're fine. How am I doing?"

•

Patient: You have got to help me, Doctor. My wife thinks she is a pretzel.
Crazy doctor: Bring her in to see me. Maybe I can straighten her out.

•

Doctor: Ask the accident victim what his name is so we can notify his family.
Nurse: He says his family knows his name.

•

Patient: Doctor, if a person's brain stops working, does he die?
Crazy doctor: How can you ask such a stupid question! You're alive, aren't you?

•

Patient: Doctor, do you think cranberries are healthy?
Crazy doctor: Well, I've never heard one complain.

•

Doctor: Deep breathing, you understand, destroys germs.
Crazy patient: Yes, Doctor, but how can I force them to breathe deeply?

# 23

## *Carter & Cora Crazy*

Carter: Do you know how long cows should be milked?
Cora: Beats me.
Carter: The same as short cows.

●

Carter: How does a crazy dentist examine a crocodile's teeth?
Cora: I can't guess.
Carter: Very carefully!

●

Carter: Why did the crazy carpenter hire a secretary?
Cora: I don't know.
Carter: To file his nails.

●

Carter: What do you call a crazy sheep who hangs out with 40 thieves?
Cora: I have no idea.
Carter: Ali Baa Baa.

●

Carter: What has an IQ of 192?
Cora: You tell me.
Carter: A group of 100 crazy people.

●

Carter: What's the easiest job in the world?
Cora: I give up.
Carter: The head of the Crazy Intelligence Agency.

●

Carter: What kills crazy flies by sitting on them?
Cora: My mind is a blank.
Carter: A fly squatter.

●

Carter: Why wouldn't the crazy lightning bolt go to the storm?
Cora: I have no idea.
Carter: Because it was on strike.

●

Carter: What happens to a crazy dog who eats table scraps?
Cora: You've got me.
Carter: He gets splinters in his tongue.

•

Carter: What is purple and a member of your family?
Cora: That's a mystery.
Carter: Your grape grandmother.

•

Carter: What did the crazy cat say when his tail got caught in the lawnmower?
Cora: Tell me.
Carter: It won't be long now.

•

Carter: What did the crazy stocking say to the needle?
Cora: I'm in the dark.
Carter: I'll be darned!

•

Carter: What did crazy Jonah say when asked how he was feeling?
Cora: Search me.
Carter: Very whale, thank you.

# 24

# *Crazy Thoughts*

Have you ever seen a ball park?

•

Did you ever see the Catskill Mountains?
*No, but I've seen them kill mice.*

•

Have you ever seen a fire fly?

•

Have you ever seen a key punch?

•

Have you ever seen a king fish?

•

Have you ever seen a ginger snap?

•

Have you ever seen a hog bristle?

•

Have you ever seen a board walk?

•

Have you ever seen a home run?

•

Have you ever seen a hot dog stand?

•

Have you ever seen a picket fence?

•

Have you ever seen a salad bowl?

•

Have you ever seen a shoe box?

•

Have you ever seen a square dance?

•

Have you ever seen a stone step?

•

Have you ever seen a tree bark?

# 25

## *Crazy Students*

I have one teacher who is so forgetful he gave the same test three weeks in a row. If he does that two more times, I may pass it.

•

Student #1: My teacher thinks I'm a perfect idiot.
Student #2: Well, she is wrong. Nobody is perfect.

•

Teacher: How long did Thomas Edison live?
Crazy student: All his life.

•

Teacher: You got a perfect zero on your exam. How did you do that?
Crazy student: It was luck. I guessed at some of the answers.

•

You can always spot an abnormal student. He is the one who comes back to school from a long vacation and remembers to bring his homework.

•

Teacher: Who can tell us something about Good Friday?
Crazy student: He was the fellow who helped Robinson Crusoe.

•

Teacher: Clay, what is the definition of "ignorance"?
Clay: I don't know.

•

Teacher: When did Napoleon die?
Crazy student: Die? I didn't even know he was sick.

•

Teacher: What do you expect to be when you get out of school?
Crazy student: An old man.

# 26

## *Christopher &*
## *Clara Crazy*

Christopher: What has three crazy feet, but no toes?
Clara: Beats me.
Christopher: A yardstick.

•

Christopher: What has crazy arms, but no hands?
Clara: I can't guess.
Christopher: A chair.

•

Christopher: Why shouldn't the crazy number 288 ever
be mentioned in mixed company?
Clara: I have no clue.
Christopher: Because it is two gross.

•

Christopher: Why did the crazy secret agent take two
aspirins and go to bed?
Clara: I don't know.
Christopher: He had a code in his head.

•

Christopher: What happened when the crazy musician died?
Clara: You've got me guessing.
Christopher: He decomposed.

•

Christopher: What did crazy Bambi put on the back of his car?
Clara: I have no idea.
Christopher: A Thumper sticker.

•

Christopher: What does a crazy veterinarian keep outside his front door?
Clara: You tell me.
Christopher: A welcome mutt.

•

Christopher: What do you have in December that you don't have in any other month?
Clara: I give up.
Christopher: The letter *D*.

•

Christopher: What do crazy jigsaw puzzles do when they get bad news?
Clara: Who knows?
Christopher: Go to pieces.

•

Christopher: What do you call a crazy pair of salesmen who go to jail?
Clara: You've got me.
Christopher: Sell-mates.

•

Christopher: What happens when you fall in love with a crazy jogger?
Clara: That's a mystery.
Christopher: You get the run-around.

•

Christopher: What would you call a crazy bird who joins the Ice Capades?
Clara: Tell me.
Christopher: A cheep skate.

•

Christopher: Why do we need the crazy reindeer?
Clara: I don't have the foggiest.
Christopher: It makes the little flowers grow.

•

Christopher: Why did the crazy secret agent whisper one, two, three, four, five, six, seven......?
Clara: It's unknown to me.
Christopher: He was a counter-spy.

•

Christopher: What crazy state doesn't feel good?
Clara: I'm in the dark.
Christopher: Ill.

•

Christopher: What grows on a tree and is terrified of
  wolves?
Clara: Search me.
Christopher: The Three Little Figs.

# 27

# *Crazy Definitions*

**Alarm clock:**
*A frightened timepiece.*

•

**Applause:**
*Two hands slapping each other's faces.*

•

**Atoll:**
*What you pay before you cross a bridge.*

•

**Author:**
*A guy who is usually write.*

•

**Bedrock:**
*Any rocks you find in your bed.*

•

**College cheer:**
*Money from home.*

•

**Finland:**
*A place where many sharks live.*

•

**Fireproof:**
*The boss's relatives.*

•

**Post Office:**
*U.S. Snail.*

•

**Flabbergasted:**
*The state you are in when you're overwhelmed by a flabber.*

•

**High heels:**
*The invention of a girl who had been kissed on the forehead one
    too many times.*

•

**Hypodermic needle:**
*A sick-shooter.*

•

**Love:**
*A heart attack.*

•

**Redskins:**
*People sunburned on the beach.*

•

**Sweater:**
*A garment worn by a small child when his mother feels chilly.*

•

**Thief:**
*A person who finds things before the owner loses them.*

•

**Twins:**
*Infant replay.*

•

**Work:**
*An unpopular way to earn money.*

# 28

# *Crazy Knock-Knock Jokes*

Knock, knock.
Who's there?
A herd.
A herd who?
A herd you were home, so I came over!

•

Knock, knock.
Who's there?
Gillette.
Gillette who?
Gillette the cat out?

•

Knock, knock.
Who's there?
Celeste.
Celeste who?
Celeste time I'll ask you.

•

Knock, knock.
Who's there?
Alfred.
Alfred who?
Alfred the needle if you'll sew on the button.

Knock, knock.
Who's there?
Amis.
Amis who?
Amis is as good as a mile.

Knock, knock.
Who's there?
Despair.
Despair who?
Despair tire is flat.

Knock, knock.
Who's there?
Radio.
Radio who?
Radio not, here I come.

•

Knock, knock.
Who's there?
Doughnut.
Doughnut who?
Doughnut open until Christmas.

•

Knock, knock.
Who's there?
Oliver.
Oliver who?
Oliver troubles will soon be over.

•

Knock, knock.
Who's there?
Yule.
Yule who?
Yule come on down, you hear?

•

Knock, knock.
Who's there?
Osborne.
Osborne who?
Osborne in the state of Georgia.

•

Knock, knock.
Who's there?
Pecan.
Pecan who?
Pecan someone your own size.

•

Knock, knock.
Who's there?
Polly Warner.
Polly Warner who?
Polly Warner cracker.

•

Knock, knock.
Who's there?
Sherwood.
Sherwood who?
Sherwood like for you to let me in.

•

Knock, knock.
Who's there?
Howard.
Howard who?
Howard you today?

•

Knock, knock.
Who's there?
Phillip.
Phillip who?
Phillip the tub so I can take a bath.

•

Knock, knock.
Who's there?
Nixon.
Nixon who?
Nixon stones will break my bones.

•

Knock, knock.
Who's there?
Sarah.
Sarah who?
Sarah doctor in the house?

•

Knock, knock.
Who's there?
Howie.
Howie who?
Fine, thanks. Howie you?

## Other Books by Bob Phillips

- World's Greatest Collection of Clean Jokes
- More Good Clean Jokes
- The Last of the Good Clean Jokes
- The Return of the Good Clean Jokes
- The All American Joke Book
- The World's Greatest Collection of Heavenly Humor
- The Best of the Good Clean Jokes
- The Best of the Good Clean Jokes Perpetual Calendar
- Wit and Wisdom
- Humor Is Tremendous
- The All-New Clean Joke Book
- Good Clean Jokes for Kids
- The Encyclopedia of Good Clean Jokes
- Ultimate Good Clean Jokes for Kids
- Awesome Good Clean Jokes for Kids
- Wacky Good Clean Jokes for Kids
- Loony Good Clean Jokes for Kids
- Bible Brainteasers
- The Ultimate Bible Trivia Challenge
- The Little Book of Bible Trivia
- How Can I Be Sure? A Pre-Marriage Inventory
- Anger Is a Choice
- Redi-Reference
- Redi-Reference Daily Bible Reading Plan
- The Delicate Art of Dancing with Porcupines
- God's Hand Over Hume
- Praise Is a Three-Lettered Word—Joy
- The Handbook for Headache Relief
- Friendship, Love & Laughter

For information on how to purchase any of the above books, contact your local bookstore or send a self-addressed stamped envelope to:

Family Services
P.O. Box 9363
Fresno, CA 93702

Dear Reader:

We would appreciate hearing from you regarding this Harvest House book. It will enable us to continue to give you the best in Christian publishing.

1. What most influenced you to purchase *Crazy Good Clean Jokes for Kids*?
   ☐ Author
   ☐ Subject matter
   ☐ Backcover copy
   ☐ Recommendations
   ☐ Cover/Title
   ☐ _____

2. Where did you purchase this book?
   ☐ Christian bookstore
   ☐ General bookstore
   ☐ Department store
   ☐ Grocery store
   ☐ Other

3. Your overall rating of this book:
   ☐ Excellent  ☐ Very good  ☐ Good  ☐ Fair  ☐ Poor

4. How likely would you be to purchase other books by this author?
   ☐ Very likely
   ☐ Somewhat likely
   ☐ Not very likely
   ☐ Not at all

5. What types of books most interest you?
   (check all that apply)
   ☐ Women's Books
   ☐ Marriage Books
   ☐ Current Issues
   ☐ Christian Living
   ☐ Bible Studies
   ☐ Fiction
   ☐ Biographies
   ☐ Children's Books
   ☐ Youth Books
   ☐ Other _____

6. Please check the box next to your age group.
   ☐ Under 18
   ☐ 18-24
   ☐ 25-34
   ☐ 35-44
   ☐ 45-54
   ☐ 55 and over

**Mail to:** Editorial Director
Harvest House Publishers
1075 Arrowsmith
Eugene, OR 97402

Name _____

Address _____

City _____ State _____ Zip _____

**Thank you for helping us to help you
in future publications!**